DIANA DAYS

Rita Grace

TABLE OF CONTENTS

Foreword

Not every woman wants to be a mistress, especially if your paramour happens to be a Prince and the eldest son of the ruling monarch.

Camilla was an exception – and you could say she fitted the Prince's lifestyle – for she was amongst the elite, a horsewoman of some repute, and intent on capturing Charles for herself. You see, there was no shame in being Camilla Shand, as she loved outdoor pursuits and was the perfect host at parties, putting everyone at ease with her charming wit and good sense of humour. Camilla had been groomed for such functions since her 'coming out.' And suffice it to say, her Prince was enamoured with her since he first caught sight of her adroitness, as she enticed him with the fact that their ancestors on both sides had fallen in love with each other. So, 'How about it?' she accosted a somewhat bemused Prince of Wales.

There was no doubt Charles was drawn to this damsel who was keen to begin a spontaneous affair from the word 'go.' You could say he was transfixed by this fair socialite who shared so many of his interests and was there waiting to become his mistress.

As for a married mistress, it was so much the better, for Charles became a married man himself – taking for his wife a fresh-faced girl in order to make her the mother of his sons, for she was just out of finishing school, virginal and attractive, and ripe for taking on the responsibility of providing heirs for the sovereign.

No-one would question his judgement, choosing Diana of shy disposition, a Spencer of renowned lineage, whose sisters were already girlfriends of this Charles Philip Arthur George, destined to be King one day.

The country was impatient for him to take a wife, none more so than his father Philip, who was anxious for him to marry and settle the constitution. But did it have to be demure Diana, chosen for her quiet disposition, untainted and brought up on the fringes of Sandringham, where she could catch Charles's roving eye as he rode across the ploughed fields next to the house?

What wasn't known then was that this Diana, would, by the 1990s, become the greatest media personality in the history of the world. Her beauty was beyond compare after she had been groomed for royalty, for she possessed the right kind of looks to make a future queen.

A kindergarten school at Pimlico was where the press first got an inkling of the girl destined to become the bride of the Prince of Wales. She had stood for the camera inadvertently with the light behind her, which exposed her long lithesome legs underneath her shimmering dress. That is how she was first snapped – a young girl of 20, with one child in her arms as another holds her hand. She was looking down – innocent, youthful and appealing. Could she have stayed that way? This awkward, upper-class young girl's downcast eyes betrayed the fact that she wasn't enjoying this at all.

Diana would be the first English woman to marry an heir to the throne for over 300 years. Her sisters had married quietly: Lady Sarah to a farmer in one of the English counties and Lady Jane to the Queen's private secretary. So the stage was set for Diana to marry, too, – the last young sister to leave Althorp House. How exciting her life was going to be! Sadly, she would be leaving her young brother Charles who was destined to be the next Earl Spencer after her loving father. The two of them had played together on the vast Althorp estate, having lost their mother who had eloped when Charles was a baby. So life would never be the same again for Lady Diana Spencer.

NO LIGHT AT THE END OF THE TUNNEL

Diana had dined on fillet of sole, Dodi on roast turbot, as they sat by candlelight in a cosy corner of the Ritz restaurant in that most romantic of cities – Paris.

They had just returned from their cruise around the Porto Cervo in Sardinia, Cap Ferret in Monte Carlo and Portofino before flying to Paris. The holiday was almost over for Diana, as she had to return to England to catch up with her boys who, by now, were in Scotland ensconced behind the walls of Balmoral with their father and grandparents.

Diana had not to hide her feelings at this new romance with Dodi, which had become a month-long holiday affair, as she was a divorced woman and could see whom she pleased without royal approval. But the paparazzi hounded her just the same, and they followed her every move the moment she stepped off the yacht with her handsome new love.

The Princess had not advised the British Embassy of her presence in France, nor had she requested any particular protection from the authorities, leaving it to Dodi to see after her safety, as it was in him she had put her faith during these last intimate occasions when the two of them had been together. He would look out for her, signalling his staff at every move they made.

The deputy security manager of the Paris Ritz happened to be Henri Paul who would drive them to their destination. No-one noticed he had drunk one or two glasses of liqueurs as he sat silently waiting for Dodi's signal, which meant a decoy car from the back of the hotel.

The two lovers got up from their table, and Dodi guided Diana to the back entrance where two bodyguards would accompany them on the short journey to Paris.

It was past midnight as the Mercedes glided away from clamouring reporters and cameramen who had spotted their getaway car and swiftly followed on revved-up motorcycles.

Which way would the Mercedes go? They would soon catch up, for this was Diana and Dodi they were chasing!

Dodi's apartment, towards the end of the Champs Elysees, was the destination for him and Diana to stay the night. The bridge over the Seine was in sight as the black racing limo sped towards the tunnel driven by an excited chauffeur, his eyes blazing as he caught reflections of the paparazzi in his wing mirror. Diana and Dodi held on to each other as the car careered into the blackness of the underground pass, as they failed to fasten their seat belts.

An almighty crash ricocheted across the expanse of the dark underpass when something went terribly wrong. The limousine had struck the central reservation pillars, which sent it spinning uncontrollably at 360 degrees, ending up a crumpled mass against the right-hand wall of the tunnel, its horn blaring and smoke pouring from the bonnet. The engine had rammed itself through the front of the car with such force that the radiator ended up in the driver's footwell. There was a smell of fuel and burning and a fear that the whole tangled heap would burst into flames.

The poor princess would have been thrown from pillar to post! The following reporters and photographers were upon the wreckage in a flash. The rear door on her side was wrenched open. The crouched Princess Diana, half kneeling, her legs buckled beneath her, was trapped in the well between the front and back seats, her head and chin pressed against her chest.

'I'm hurt,' she was heard to say to the one reporter who had dared to peep into the inferno. Luckily, a doctor was passing by at the time of the accident, and he went to her aid in the dimly lit tunnel. He rushed back to his car for oxygen and medical equipment, and when he returned, Diana was crying out again:-

'Oh my God! — Leave me alone, leave me alone.'

She repeatedly said how much she hurt as the doctor gently put a resuscitation mask on her mouth. It was then she lost consciousness, and within six minutes, the emergency services arrived on the scene.

It was almost one o'clock by the time Diana was released from the wreckage and rushed to the Pitié-Salpêtrière Hospital within the shadow of the Eiffel Tower. Would that she could make it through the night! The surgeons fought desperately to save her, opening up her chest and massaging her heart, but it was to no avail as the princess had sustained a wound to the upper left pulmonary vein, together with rapture to the pericardium. It was assumed Diana was sideways at the moment of impact, most probably glancing backwards to see if the so-called 'rat-pack' were following.

Unknown to her, her companion Dodi had died beside her almost immediately. The Princess was pronounced dead at 4 a.m. The only survivor was Trevor Rees-Jones, the bodyguard who happened to have fastened his seat belt but who had also sustained terrible injuries.

It was Sunday, the 31st of August 1997, and Diana was dead. How many hearts would she be breaking now that hers had stopped? Who was to tell the world and unravel the terrible tragedy? And who would dress her a final time for her coffin? Everyone was shaking with shock and grief. How could our Diana have died?

Those wee small hours – hadn't they a tale to tell? The desperate fight to save her life – the heart massage that failed to set that racing heart aflame once more! That vital oxygen just couldn't get through, and our sacred Queen of Hearts was doomed to die without regaining consciousness. She had suffered a massive heart attack and died on the operating table. The doctors gave a sigh of despair and mopped their sweating brows. How could this fine-looking young woman who lay before them be the Princess of Wales?

Dying Diana had been discovered in the mangled Mercedes

with her arm around Dodi Al Fayed. It is said the driver, Henri Paul, lost control of the car as it flipped over seven times after crashing into the 13th pillar of the Alma underpass. The unmistakable face of Diana laid motionless amid the carnage of the concertina-like wreckage that was billowing acrid smoke further into the tunnel.

Two of the inmates of the car were already dead – the driver, Henri Paul, and Diana's date, Dodi, who had both suffered ruptured aortas and fractured spines, together with neck and back injuries resulting from a head-on crash at 96mph. It was exceptional for a patient who had suffered such serious intra-thoracic lesions, such as Diana had endured, to reach the hospital alive. Amid all the hassle, Trevor Rees-Jones was fighting for his life, too.

'She is alive,' shouted Romuald Rat as he approached the smoking Mercedes and took the princess's pulse after he had opened the door to where she was sitting. He spoke in English – 'The doctor is on his way.' Fortunately, the doctor appeared on the scene along with the reporters and photographers, and they made way for him to attend Diana. Dr. Mailliez returned to his car for an oxygen mask and pressed it to the ashen face of the princess as she closed her eyes on the scene. Amidst the flashes of the photographers' cameras, this doctor had given Diana light in the dark tunnel!

Dr Mailliez could not remember anything the princess might have said during her ordeal. In fact, he did not know who this person he was treating was. He just hoped the doctors at the hospital would save her life as she looked so young and beautiful. Her beau had died – that was for sure – and he did not know that he was the son of Mohammed Al Fayed, the famed Egyptian who owned the Paris Ritz as well as other well-to-do places. In the front of the mangled car, the chauffeur and badly injured bodyguard were masked by the billowing air bags that had proved virtually useless against the massive impact of the crash, although the bodyguard was showing some signs of life, strapped in as he was by his seat belt.

'What noble heart was here undone,' Lord Byron would have said. Would it be that this damsel had to die at the same age as he was when he died all too soon at just 36 years old! Byron had been a cult figure in his day; the same as Diana in our day. Their characters may have been similar, though Byron behaved far worse and wantonly than Diana ever did. These prophetic and exquisite words of Lord Byron could serve as the epitaph for both :-

'So we'll go no more a roving – so late into the night
Though the heart be still as loving – and the moon be still as bright'

Poor Diana, her heart had been crushed, her soul destroyed as her boys were waiting for her to return to her homeland. Her sons, William and Harry, had been her world, and they would be shattered by the tragic news – the most profound piece of news ever – that their mother had died. How could it be – their own mum, the Princess of Wales having her life cut short in such a tragic way?
Prince Charles had woken the boys in their deepest slumber. To tell them of their dear mother's plight was the hardest thing he had ever to impart.

'Their mum Diana, with the downcast eyes Had entered the tunnel and met her demise'

The Queen expressed her own sorrow by exclaiming, 'Diana was an exceptional and gifted human being; in good times and bad, she never lost her capacity to smile and laugh, nor to inspire others with her warmth and kindness. I share in your determination to cherish her memory.'
Masses of flowers of every colour and hue were brought to the entrance of Kensington Palace, the Princess's London home. The crowds swelled into four-deep queues in a desperate attempt to lay

their bunches of orchids, lilies, sunflowers, and every conceivable posy you could mention, until an impromptu shrine was being created before everyone's eyes. Candles and teddies were backing up dangerously on the pavement, together with well-wishers' letters and cards and heart-rending poems for their princess, for the people loved Diana like no other and made sure the palace knew it.

This woman had given the country an heir to the throne, and although she was divorced from the sovereign's son, she had continued to be passionate about the well-being of the poor, the deprived and the downtrodden. Diana had achieved her stated aim when she had flown to Angola to highlight the landmines campaign. She had remembered a little girl who had had her intestines blown out, and she knew she could do something by being amongst the badly injured who had had limbs blown off, especially the children, and she had committed herself to the cause.

Now that she was dead, her devoted butler took to France the last dress she would be seen in, a simple black affair she had recently acquired. He sat at the side of her coffin in St James's Palace throughout the night before the funeral.

Diana's lead-lined casket weighed 40 stone, and it had been Prince Charles and her two sisters accompanying it back to London, draped in the royal standard.

The Princess's divorce had only become absolute a year before her death. It was then she became Diana, Princess of Wales, without 'Her Royal Highness' distinction. Her family, the Spencers, was peeved that the Queen should denude her of her full title, but in the meantime, she could continue to live at Kensington Palace and have access to her boys whenever she liked.

A former woman of the slums of Albania happened to die on the eve of Diana's funeral. She was none other than Mother Theresa who had forged a deep bond with Diana after they supported the same humanitarian causes. Mother Theresa had become a naturalised

Indian and spoke Bengali, and she was not amiss at extracting funds from crooks and despots, not batting an eyelid when the money was meant for a good cause.

Now this was Diana's funeral we were witnessing on that clammy September morning that had all London lining the route of the procession. The sight of the hearse filled everyone with remorse. Cameras loomed in and focused on the one white rosette that bore the name 'Mummy' and was written by Prince Harry himself.

The cortege approached Buckingham Palace where the Princess had once captivated the hearts of the nation on her wedding to Prince Charles and where she had kissed him on the balcony to the terrific roar of the crowds. Now it was a far more solemn occasion as the hearse crept past the palace gates with the Princess being mourned on a scale that had never been seen before. Festoons of flowers were thrown as her coffin left Westminster Abbey and made its way to Diana's final resting place. It was quite a good way off, as Althorp Park was in Northampton, and the main royal party would have to make their way partly by train.

It had been an even more solemn affair within the Abbey itself when Earl Spencer gave his speech about his sister, as he paid tribute to Diana's compassion for the common people and caused bitterness by castigating the Queen for stripping the Princess of her HRH title.

And so, Diana was swept away to heaven on a floodtide of flowers. Her ancestral home at Althorp would be the final resting place for someone like her with natural nobility, who was classless and proved that she needed no royal title to generate her particular brand of magic.

So just who was this damsel of distress – this Diana who had captured the hearts of all the world and once had a prince kneeling at her feet? How was it that she had got into this new partnership and suffered as a consequence? Just who were we paying this last great tribute to? From whence had she come?

SHY 'DI'

Lady Diana Spencer was born on the first day of July 1961 and was the third child of the 8th Earl Spencer and his good lady Frances, daughter of Lady Fermoy, who was a lady-in-waiting to the Queen Mother. It was at Park House on the Queen's Sandringham Estate where all the Spencer babies were born – two elder sisters before Diana and then Charles, the youngest who was mothered by Diana as he grew up.

> Earl Spencer had three daughters fair
> The younger one to show much flair

I think you could say that Lady Diana, as she was then, was an aristocrat to her fingertips and was accustomed to having her whims indulged, especially by her father whom she adored. Her sisters, Lady Sarah and Lady Jane, were very much together and attracted the attention of the royals who were near neighbours in this lovely part of Norfolk. As children, the Spencer girls were used to seeing the Windsor boys, and they would play together on the vast estate.

It was to Diana that her mother gave her own name, Frances, and hoped her little girl would show grace and poise, as Diana loved pretty clothes and enjoyed going to parties. In fact, she had hopes of becoming a ballerina and Frances gave her every encouragement.

When her brother Charles came along, Diana loved to be with him, and the two of them became soul mates, running around the Park House and sharing their love of the outdoors. But something was about to happen to spoil that contentment. The rowing of their parents upset the solitude of the house, as the young twosome listened intently, hiding on the stairway in case they should be spotted. As the rows got louder and louder, they put their hands to their ears and hoped it would go away, but before long, a divorce was in the making when their mother packed her bags and ran to the arms of another man. Diana was only six, and so began her role of being the comforter and protector of her young brother until it was time for her to take her place at Silfield School in King's Lynn. You could understand her not settling very well as she was missing her mother as well as her young sibling, and it was as if her childhood had been shattered by unforeseen circumstances. But she still had her father when she needed him, and the two of them shared a special bond after her mother left.

Diana was no scholar, and her brother, being more of a swot, ridiculed his sister for being an 'airhead.' He even nicknamed her 'Brian' after the dim-witted snail in the children's TV show 'The Magic Roundabout.' No matter how much she tried, Diana could not be as clever as her brother who showed great promise in the schoolroom.

When Lady Diana was sent to Riddlesworth Hall, she was still painfully shy and lonely at being away from home at this boarding school near Diss in Norfolk. Maybe it was then she started to feel compassion for others in the same position as herself, as she felt hopeless and like a drop-out. 'I'm as thick as a plank,' she professed, 'with a brain the size of a pea.'

Of course, she could have been homesick for her family, as by now, her parents had divorced, and she longed for the closeness of her near brother as her sisters seemed to be a world away. Matters only got worse when she eventually followed her sisters to West Heath, the all-girls public school near Sevenoaks in Kent, where she failed to gain a single successful examination. Diana failed her O levels, too, even though she sat for them twice. All this led to her leaving school at 16. This was not to say she had failed at everything as she excelled in sports, particularly swimming, netball, and tennis. Plus, she was poised to take up tap-dancing and ballet for which she showed great promise.

Earl Spencer, who was by now well ensconced at Althorp House, the Spencer family seat in Northamptonshire, saw to it that Diana had a brief stay at the Institut Alpin Videmanette, an expensive Swiss finishing school where she gained confidence and deportment. After that, she was in line for a fine flat in Coleherne Court near Kensington, which she would share with her three best girlfriends. Here, she was at her happiest and was free to do as she pleased. Surely, she thought, she had reached her zenith and could pick and choose her employment, be it scrubbing floors for the rich or taking care of their offspring. She opted for the latter and became an assistant in a kindergarten in Pimlico. My! How the public would take notice of this nice new nursemaid in the months to come, for at last, m'lady was going somewhere!

The clicking cameras had never had it so good in this busy part of London, catching Lady Diana as she departed from Coleherne Court and following her all the way to Pimlico. 'Why?' – you may ask. Because she happened to be the subject of speculation as a suitable partner for the prominent Prince of Wales. They had been seeing each other in secret, and it was 'Shy Di' the Prince wanted for a bride.

The first inkling of a romance between Prince Charles and Lady Diana Spencer was when the Daily Mail's Nigel Dempster printed a picture of Diana and headed it, 'Has Charles discovered his future bride?', which was in September 1980. Everyone sought to enquire of her status and reputation, as she was just nineteen and fresh from finishing school. It had been her elder sister Sarah who was mostly connected with Charles, as they had spent several skiing holidays together, with the newspapers following them up the ski slopes, wondering whether there was a romance. As it turned out, Sarah Spencer went on to marry Mr McCorquodale, a farmer, and eventually retired to the countryside. It was thought young Diana was meant for Prince Andrew, as they had been drawn together often during their adolescence. She also posed as Prince Edward's girlfriend, being more his age.

But no, folk got it wrong. Lady Diana only had eyes for Charles as she sat with him one day commiserating over the death of his favourite uncle, Earl Mountbatten, who had been blown up on his boat. 'You should be with someone who can look after you,' she said solemnly, thinking to herself 'that someone should be me.' Yes. She could upstage her sisters and make the Prince her own, as she had the looks and determination to do it.

Diana's father had become Earl Spencer following on from those early Spencers who were viscounts in the king's service. The 5th earl had held office as first lord of the admiralty and also served as viceroy in Ireland, and the 6th earl was the Rt.Hon. Charles Robert Spencer KG, GCVO who became Lord Chamberlain and was eventually raised to the peerage as Lord Althorp.

The founding father of the family had been one Sir John Spencer, born as far back as 1533. He was a Tudor farmer who became the richest of the Elizabeth 'sheep masters' and was the first to market his flock direct to London.

Even Charles could be traced back as being in the Spencers' blood line, reportedly being the 'good looking king with the pronounced locks.'

And so, Diana could hardly be called a 'commoner' when picked to become the bride of the Queen's firstborn son. As she herself announced, 'I am used to the royal family and so it should not be a problem.' After all, she had lived next door to them when they were holidaying at Sandringham and romping around with the boys in particular. Her sisters and brother Charles were also 'in the gang.'

What had mesmerized Prince Charles about this youngest sister was the fact of her being the noisiest of the three. He thought Diana the most charming and spontaneous of the Spencer girls, so she was beginning to be seen more and more by his side. It was particularly noticed that she had attended one of his polo matches and was also spotted at the Braemar gathering in the Highlands and was seen taking the afternoon flight back to London with Sir Nicholas Soames who was Charles's Equerry. Yes, even though she was blossoming into an impressive young woman, she had become an important appendage to the Prince, and photographers could see the romance gaining ground.

Very soon, Diana would become public property and her life would never be the same again. The eyes of the world would be focused on her, and her happy giggling days with her friends would soon be over. How sad that she could not be her own private self any more now that the Prince was about to call! Her days of languishing in obscurity were over for good.

> The youngest of three daughters fair
> She attracted Charles into her lair
> A fresh-plucked flower – so rare

This was the child who so wanted to become a ballerina but who had lassoed the Prince of Wales for herself. She was chosen for her politeness more than anything, and Charles was fascinated by her country-fresh good looks and wholesome features. She had only to flash those vivid blue eyes and he was more or less hypnotized. He would make her the most famous face of the century. And on her finger would be the finest sapphire ring to match those beautiful downcast eyes!

> 'Charming for Charles, and so carefree – A beautiful bride she
> would be'

Poor Diana – her background would be portrayed as her having come from a broken home: Frances, her mother, had left her father, now Lord Althorp, for another man. That man happened to be Peter

Shand-Kydd of wallpaper fame, who had lured Diana's mother away from her father when she left abruptly to go and live with him. Frances had sought custody of the two younger members of the family, Diana and her little brother Charles, but grandmother Fermory put her spoke in and ordered the judge to let them stay with their father. Of course, Diana and Charles were not aware of what was going on during the turmoil, as they were safely ensconced at Althorp where they continued to play and exercise their childhood.

What was gruelling for their mother had been the loss of her baby the year before Diana was born. The children had become weapons in an unstable marriage, and undeniably, Diana suffered the consequences. She mothered little Charles all the more after their mother left. The animosity had hardened her resolve to do as well as she could in class, but she was distracted by the events at home. She most probably felt unloved and sought recourse with members of the Althorp staff, as she would often go down to the kitchens to see what they were up to and help herself to whatever they were cooking. It was an opulent establishment though Diana was not at all happy in herself. It was not the same as being at Sandringham, as Althorp was large and foreboding for an aspiring young girl of Diana's disposition.

As she reached her teens, Diana got to love gossip and enjoyed giggling at naughty jokes. She would tease her school friends, as by now, her sisters were grown up and began attracting the opposite sex, which was expected of noble families such as the Spencers had become. Sister Jane was in line for marrying the Queen's private secretary, Robert Fellowes, and Diana was called upon to be one of her bridesmaids. The 8th Earl Spencer was proud to be giving his middle daughter away to a prominent member of the Queen's staff.

Diana loved to be growing up and sharing a flat with her three best friends – Ann Bolton, Carolyn Pride, and Virginia Pittman. They took turns to fetch the milk and collect the morning papers. Of course, the secret they all shared was that their flatmate Diana was seeing the Prince of Wales, and they were sworn to secrecy. The Spencer girl was keen to take a job with small children and began to drive back and forth to her employment at the Young England Kindergarten school in Pimlico. She just seemed an awkward upper-class young girl going about her business when the press began to take notice. From now on, there was no escape for Diana as she tried to tackle the cameraman bent on taking her picture on each and every journey. She would settle for them taking one picture of her outside of the nursery to quell their obsession. What a mistake this turned out to be!

'Diana of the downcast eyes' became the young damsel's trademark as she tried to avoid the flashing camera bulbs. Quite inadvertently, she had posed with the light behind her, and there for all to see were her exposed long, slender legs from behind the diaphanous dress she was wearing, with one child in her arms and another holding her hand

'Whatever will people think,' thought Diana, not having realized that her summer skirt was so revealing as to show everything underneath. It was as if she had been set up, as all the papers went ahead and published without fear of retribution.

> Diaphanous Di looked terribly shy
> As she posed outside for a picture
> Her eyes looked down – not up at the sky
> As the lens moved in to take her

All the same, Diana appeared beautiful and beguiling, although becomingly shy, her mop of fair hair framing her fine features. Of noble birth she truly was, and her informality and compassion shone forward from this first photograph. It was no wonder she chose 'I vow to thee my country' for her forthcoming wedding to the Prince, as she pledged herself to the people as well at such a young age.

The Stuff of Fairy Tales

Diana was setting a precedent – being a young bride at the end of her teens, but she was loving every minute of the preparation. She showed off her €30,000 engagement ring and explained Charles had first proposed in the cabbage patch of an old friend's country house. Later, of course, he proposed officially at Windsor Castle, and in due course, the couple posed for pictures on the steps of Buckingham Palace. They were all beams and smiles as the press enquired if they were in love. 'Of course,' Diana politely replied whilst the Prince answered in a hushed tone, 'Whatever love is,' as if wanting to dodge the question completely. Diana's eyes lifted up to reveal her sparkling blue eyes, which matched the large sapphire in her ring, as well as her blue two-piece suit, and the photographers snapped away, as these pictures would get worldwide coverage for such an important announcement.

No longer would Diana be the sixties child – full of intense excitement at trying on new dresses, albeit ones which didn't suit her, such as the diaphanous skirt that exposed her legs. She was now in line to have her very own dresser and designer in the form of Catherine Walker who had moved to Britain after earning a doctorate in aesthetics. Although she was an intense, reclusive woman, she had come a long way from selling clothes out of a basket in the King's Road. Becoming an expert pattern cutter, fitter and seamstress, Catherine started her own company as she had a keen eye for detail. Through contacts with Diana's hairdresser, she was soon called upon to make the Princess's clothes, and from then on, Diana was seen in Catherine Walker gowns for all her glittering occasions, as she had become Diana's favourite designer.

Of course, it had been left to the Emmanuels to create Diana's wedding dress – a husband and wife partnership that worked tirelessly to be in time for the royal wedding. Every time the Princess-to-be went for a fitting, she had lost pounds and the dress had to be altered accordingly.

Diana had got wedding nerves in the weeks coming up to the July state occasions and seemed to have lost a considerable amount of weight. When she finally appeared in the dress, she was absolutely swallowed beneath layers of the taffeta ivory silk that flounced about and crinkled under the summer sunshine. Its enormous train took some handling as the Princess's bridesmaids tried to grapple with it. The dress had frills that plunged at the neckline and puff sleeves that hid Diana's painfully thin arms. To use Diana's words, 'It was the most emotionally confusing day of my life.' The Prince looked charming in his Royal Navy uniform and failed to notice Diana's distress in the weight of her dress. Hundreds of people lined the route to catch a glimpse of Diana emerging from the glass coach. Both parties had fluffed their lines at the ceremony, getting their names in the wrong order, but the Archbishop put them at their ease by explaining they were 'the stuff of fairy tales.'

The couple would be following in the footsteps of the Queen and the Duke of Edinburgh by spending the first few days of their honeymoon at Broadlands, the home of the Mountbattens. Their twelve years difference in age was beginning to show, as Charles had packed his fishing rods and several books to read! In no time, the new princess was beginning to feel like the 'prisoner of Wales.' Maybe he was already tired of 'her noise' and did not crave the excitement of his young wife. The peace and quiet of Broadlands tempted the prince to take up his painting, much to the annoyance of his young bride who craved his undivided attention at such a crucial stage in their honeymoon. Could he not see that the blushing bride by his side was now 'the Princess of Wales? Yes, Diana wanted her Prince desperately, as she loved him more than anything and wanted his whole attention.

There seemed to be something niggling at the back of her new husband's mind that distracted him when they were alone together. And Diana needed pampering more than ever if she were ever to fit in with his way of life and that of the royal family. He could be her teacher in readiness for her new role – or so Diana thought!

But Charles was distant and wrapped up in his own emotions. That was when Diana had an inkling that there might be someone else involved in his life. It grieved her deeply to think she wasn't the real love of his life. How could he not love her when she was giving her all, thrust as she was into the limelight of a world she knew little about? What was expected of her now that she was the Princess of Wales? A good deal more than she was prepared to admit, it seemed, as no help was coming from the royals to help her deal with her situation.

The new Princess wished she had stayed the way she was before her prince came to call, as the pressures he brought to bear taxed her energies to the limit. How could she be expected to change from the ordinary girl she was to face the onslaught of the world's press in her new role? It could not happen overnight. Would her sisters be of any help? She called on her sister Sarah who had been Prince Charles's girlfriend before ever she was. But Sarah could not help her, as she herself was now married with young children. She had left the lights of London for a farm outpost on the borders of Lincolnshire and loved her new life away from the pressure of the big city. Diana visited her quite often and longed for the same contentment.

Diana's mother, now Mrs Shand-Kidd, also had opted to live in Scotland where she could keep a small profile and not be the subject of ridicule, as her second marriage had failed, and now, she was all alone without the comfort of her grown-up family. Lord Althorp had married again, which did not meet the approval of Diana and her sisters. His wife was none other than Raine, daughter of Barbara Cartland, the lady always in the pink and forever in print! Yet Raine became the driving force at Althorp, and the Earl had to make changes to accommodate her wishes. It was no wonder the family began to call her 'acid Raine', as they just could not stomach her. Even so, she made their father happy and so the family put up with her antics. Barbara Cartland thought it a high honour to have Diana as her daughter's stepchild and was always the one to heap high regard on Diana's suitability as Prince Charles's wife.

The news was good – a few months into the marriage, Diana found herself pregnant and feeling sick with it. She had been losing weight and cutting short her engagements whilst she caught up with her new condition. Charles was pleased with the prospect of becoming a father. When William was born, they were both ecstatic, and Diana was so proud to show him off to the cameras. She took time off to be a mother and would love to have stayed at home all the time with him. A tour of Australia was on the cards, and she insisted on taking William with them. It turned out to be a big success, as Diana could give William a cuddle when she had done with her engagements. She still looked pitifully thin and strained, and everyone wondered if she had the slimmer's disease, bulimia nervosa.

In fact, she was suffering from stress and taking it out on her body, starving herself during the day and binging at night when no-one was looking. It was a cry for help but no-one was listening, especially not Prince Charles. He began to think she had some sort of mental disorder.

Diana was thinking, 'What if he doesn't love me any more?' She had given birth to their son and had been at his side at functions she wasn't even interested in. Inside, she was feeling anxious and unloved and only secure in her love for little William whom she adored. 'Why didn't Prince Charles feel the same?' she wondered. He wanted the Princess to be seen by his side, and so she acceded, becoming more and more the most important and beautiful woman on the land. People craved her presence and she was overcome by all the attention. She had to look her best even though she did not feel up to it, and there was a limit to her capabilities. Eventually the bulimia took control of her, and she just got thinner and thinner. This was no detriment to her courtiers, as they loved to dress her the way she was – stick thin and a size 8. Yes, Diana was every designer's dream. She knew just how to put a veil over her anxieties and appear a peerless person putting a brave face on things. Her expertly applied make-up masked any unhappiness she might have been experiencing. Right from the pale blusher on her cheeks to the ivory-toned foundation, Diana looked the perfect English rose. Her complexion, complimented by strawberry-pink lip gloss, blue eyeliner and the obligatory mascara, presented her as the shimmering beauty she truly was. Her crop of thick hair seemed to be her best feature, as it could be teased into so many easy styles to suit the fashion of the day. Her hairdresser just had to highlight it a little to blend in with her English rose complexion.

Indeed, the thickness of Diana's hair proved to be her crowning glory, as it could be layered into smoothness to fit neatly under her hats.

A Spencer girl – tall and fair
Highlights shining from her hair

No-one could match Diana's haute couture, as she had become the fashion icon of the twentieth century. Hers was the face to launch a thousand ships, and her figure flattered every magazine on the newsagent's stand. Talk about a popular princess – you could not fault her in the slightest, as she strove hard to keep her place at the top of the glamour stakes. You could say she kept herself slim and toned by swimming every morning, as this was her favourite sport.

Diana had not looked so great when she first met the prince, and she talked candidly about still being in nappies when Charles first knew of her existence. 'I made a lot of noise and he seemed to like that,' she revealed. 'Of course, he was seeing my sister before he ever considered me, as all I did was lounge around the place, fearless and fat, and without make-up. It came as quite a shock when he looked at me twice.' Diana was pleasantly surprised by the Prince's attention and remarked, 'Marrying into the royal family won't be a problem.' She happened to address that remark to a nearby reporter when he caught her and Charles alone together, wrestling with binoculars that hung around the prince's neck. Of course, she was still a teenager, and it was pure speculation to think Charles was serious about this sweet girl with the downcast eyes. Clearly, they could laugh together and have fun, it seemed.

It would be another couple of years before Diana was packed off to live with the Queen Mother at Clarence House, as she was clearly 'the one' when Charles had made his mind up. The gracious queen mum would take Diana under her wing and prepare her for becoming a royal bride. After all, it had long been assumed that she and Diana's grandmother had hatched the whole charade! 'My Diana would be good for Charles,' Lady Fermoy might have advised! The queen mum took her at her word.

Or maybe it was Prince Philip who urged his son to find a wife by hinting it was high time. Poor Charles just could not win either way, and who was his father to give him his orders? It had come to something when the heir to the throne was being forced into wedlock against his own wishes. What everyone really wanted to know was 'who would he choose?'

At the bottom of his heart, Prince Charles loved another, and he had kept it secret for a number of years, as this lady had gone and married someone else in the meantime. She was probably sick of waiting for him to ask her. He had had girlfriends galore and must have been ticking them off, one at a time, until his pencil stopped at 'Diana.' She was the one he finally chose to take on the task of his burdensome future.

Diana was both surprised and shocked that Charles had chosen her over all his other girlfriends, as she thought them far superior to herself in both intelligence and wit. But her politeness and natural loveliness appealed to the 32-year-old Prince who would make her his princess before the year was out.

She liked her poise
He liked her noise

The couple would be poised to live in a palace for the rest of their lives. Kensington was the residence of the royals and would go down well with Diana, as she liked to shop on the High Street and at nearby Knightsbridge. Princess Margaret and the Duchess of Gloucester would be their near neighbours.

A Good-looking Guards Officer

The Queen Mum and Lady Fermoy knew Diana would make a good mother, and they talked about her on their 'get-togethers' at Clarence House. Little William was soothed by his mum putting her little finger in his mouth, as this would stop him fussing whilst the royals sat for photo sessions with this latest addition to the family. He was a good boy on the whole, and Diana would not want him to be mollycoddled, which was the royal fashion when Charles had been a baby. He would be having a nanny soon enough, but Diana wanted to be his sole protector whilst he was so very small.

Diana would be rewarded for her loyalty in good time by the way of jewellery from the Queen's own inheritance – an art deco diamond and emerald necklace that had belonged to an earlier monarch who happened to be Queen Mary, the Queen's grandmother. Later on, Diana would be entrusted with the Lover's Knot Tiara of pearls and diamonds for grand occasions. But where was Diana's palace where she could sit and wear the crown?

There had been contemplation for some time for a place for Diana and Charles to call their own. They finally opted for Highgrove, a country mansion near Tetbury in Gloucestershire. They could commute quite quickly from their London residence, and of course, what did distance matter when you drove a Mercedes SL as Diana did? Charles could settle down and grow his own produce as organically as possible and Diana could entertain her guests in opulent style.

By now she was heavily pregnant with her second child, another boy as it turned out, and William would have a playmate. Unfortunately, Diana suffered post-natal depression, which put a damper on things. Try as she might, she just could not get into her stride. What should have been triumphant weekends away with her children at Highgrove turned out to be miserable wet weekends to be put up with rather than enjoyed, as far as she was concerned. She failed to see the beauty of the place and longed to be back in familiar Kensington and Knightsbridge where the shops were lit up and where she felt at home. Charles got down to the task of transforming Highgrove Gardens and was at his happiest growing all kinds of vegetables and fruits for the farmhouse kitchens. What wife would not appreciate all his efforts?

It became 'Wills and Harry,' the royal children, and they brought a breath of spring into the royal nursery. Harry had a mop of rusty hair and looked more a Spencer boy than a Windsor. Diana had failed to gain weight after two pregnancies, which was to be expected when she was on the go all the time. She had to have fittings for this and that occasions, and her dressers did what they could to cloak her thinness. What was to become of this greatest media personality if she became too frail for her frocks?

Her boys were growing up quickly and wanted new recreations. Riding, football, rugby – this was what was expected of boys. This would put Diana in the position of employer, as she sought tactful men to teach her youngsters. As for Charles, he had become rather estranged of late, and so Diana was forced to admit that he had a mistress somewhere! Who could she be?

Not only was Diana's marriage in trouble but so was her sister-in-law's, the Duchess of York, who, like Diana, had come from a common background to marry Prince Andrew, the Queen's second son. Sarah Ferguson was soon nicknamed 'Fergie,' as everyone loved her freedom of spirit, and she had lovely titian-coloured hair to match her fiery temperament. There were soon four royal children, as Fergie gave birth to two girls, and so the two royal princes had founded new dynasties. There were royal get-togethers at Buckingham Palace and Windsor Castle and, come Christmas, Sandringham House. Fergie's girls were named Beatrice and Eugenie and appeared on the royal Christmas cards. Both Royal Highnesses were proud of their children.

The Queen now had six grandchildren altogether, as Princess Anne had been the first to marry, have a daughter and a son and lived at Gatcombe Park in Gloucestershire. What a fiasco it was when all three royal marriages were doomed to failure! Princess Anne, whose marriage to Mark Phillips ended in divorce, quietly got wed again, without any fuss, and remains to this day less a source of embarrassment than her brothers.

Of course, both Diana and Fergie became the best of friends, being married to the Queen's sons and adopting the royal way of life. Fergie possessed a buxom figure and longed to be slim like Diana. The press castigated her for her dress sense and hoped she would follow Diana's example and become a fashion icon. But Fergie wanted to be her own woman and would not conform to what the 'old guard' at Buckingham Palace expected of her. Andrew just loved her the way she was and did not want her to change, and when the girls were born, he was the usual doting father, giving his wife his utmost loyalty and support. She began to be known as 'Fergie, the Freebie Duchess,' as she liked to spend oceans of money and go on holidays countless times. On one of those holidays, she met a Count and was rumoured to be in love with him. Andrew went his own way, complete with cameras, and forged a new career after serving on helicopters in the Royal Navy. Later he took up golf, hoping to trim down from the heavyweight he had become. After all, he was sometimes referred to as the 'Duke of Pork.'

After Fergie had got heavily into debt, it was expected the Queen would bail her out, but she stuck to her guns and tried to earn her living writing children's books, amongst other things such as joining slimming clubs and becoming a talk host. She had a lot of success in America and was spending as much time there as in England. The Duke and Duchess of York stayed friends after their separation and were always in the company of their daughters, Beatrice and Eugenie.

Fergie, like Diana, had never had any lessons on how to be royal, and she let it be known that the only thing they advised her to do was to wave more slowly.

Now the Queen had two wayward daughters-in-law. How was she expected to cope with them? They were even threatening not to attend Sandringham House at Christmas. The two women were becoming bored with protocol and felt stifled. Diana would not want to wear the royal jewellery. She had come into the royal circle with nothing but a single string of pearls and a gold 'D' charm on a choker that her school friends had bought her on her 16th birthday. Her dear father had given her an empty jewel case as a wedding gift but she had failed to fill it. Her clothes were her future from now on, and all the haute couture houses fought for her, as she had the figure to die for. She became something, this Diana, when Charles threw her over for his mistress. She would show the world she was the best-dressed woman of the century. Even Versace was at her beck and call. He would design her the most revealing dresses that made their own statement. 'Just look at me,' Diana was saying.

She would attract the attention of several young men who casually came to call. One was a good-looking Guards Officer, with auburn hair and a pronounced stride about his person. He had come to teach Wills and Harry how to ride. Diana became infatuated with him, so much so, that she began an affair. He lived with his mum in Devonshire, and she would spend the weekends with him in his hideaway surroundings. When he was called away, she wrote love letters to him and begged him a safe return. Diana never realised she could be so much in love. The Prince could turn a blind eye as he had more than his hands full at the time – full of his fancy piece – a certain Camilla Parker Bowles. Uncannily, she had been in contact with the Prince since well before his marriage. She was the lady who waited in vain for a chance to marry him herself. Diana was seething when she found out the truth about her husband. What had she done to deserve such dishonesty, when she had been a chaste loyal bride on her wedding day?

Camilla loomed large in the Prince's life
Though Diana didn't know it
Their long romance had been so rife
So Di took up with Hewitt

Charles and Camilla both shared a passion for riding, which left Diana in the doldrums as she had fallen off her pony when she was a girl, and it had put her off horses for good. She had been 10 years old and had broken her arm.

Camilla could not wait for Prince Charles to propose and so married Brigadier Andrew Parker Bowles, to whom she had become engaged in 1973. Charles was shy at coming forward in asking for her hand and lost her in the process. As it was, they were both in their mid-twenties and would have made a fine match. It seems ironic that both Camilla and Charles said goodbye to their marriages in the same year – that of 1996.

In the absence of Diana, Charles had to find a chaperone for his boys when he went on holiday and spent time with them. She came in the guise of Tiggy Legge-Bourke, a socialite of some standing, which infuriated Diana. 'Why should someone be taking care of my boys and even going on vacation with them?' she sighed. But Charles needed someone of Tiggy's disposition, and William and Harry became quite fond of her as she was a good sport. Henceforth, the Prince, his good friend Tiggy, and the two young princes were seen everywhere together, which made Diana feel right out of it. But she buried her anxieties and concentrated on her new love, the captain who came a-courting her. Tiggy became another target of her unhappiness, as she was suspicious of her intentions, albeit innocent as they were, as she just wanted the young Princes to enjoy themselves in her company. Ziggy was not short of giving large bear-hugs, and as she became more and more accepted, would tickle them to death. Of course, William and Harry lapped it up, and you could tell from their expressions that they were enjoying being in Tiggy's care. The boys were not growing up in the 'Windsor mould' as Diana suspected but quite the opposite – unrestrained and allowed to be themselves. William, in particular, had developed an inherent kindness to all those around him and loved to put people at their ease when they met him. Harry was a little young to understand his parents' quarrels, and he joined his brother in having a good time when they were together. Tiggy resumed her role of protector of the two and drove them up hill and down in the knowledge that she was approved of by the Prince of Wales.

William began to look more like Diana with every passing day, and he also possessed her sensitivity and kindness. Naturally, he was embarrassed at his parents' marital difficulties and hoped they would sort things out between them. He sought solace from his cousin Peter Phillips, Princess Anne's son who was four years older and had gone through the same hostilities of his parents. Diana was pleased with this relationship, as she trusted Peter when he became William's bosom pal.

William and Harry were at school at Ludgrove when Diana had to break the news to them that she and their father were separating. She told them that, although she still loved their Papa, she could not continue living under the same roof as him. Wills wept silently at the news and hugged his mother tightly, whilst Harry bent his head and said nothing. Underneath they had been expecting things to come to a head, as they were just two boys undergoing their education, the older one eleven and his young brother just eight. How sad it was for them.

Diana would want the world to know of her unhappiness, as she planned a secret meeting with the BBC programme 'Panorama,' in which she revealed her hidden anxieties at having become the Princess of Wales and found to her displeasure that her husband loved another woman. 'There are three of us in this marriage,' she confessed. Of course, the palace was furious at such outrageous allegations, and even more so, when the Princess confessed that she had taken a lover, too, out of her unhappiness. She went on to explain how her depression had led to wanting to take her own life – of slitting her wrists and harming herself by slashing her arms. Bulimia nervosa erupted out of her neurosis, and she did not know which way to turn. Everyone was shocked and sympathized with the Princess, for had she not become the greatest media personality in the history of the globe? Yes indeed, she had become 'The People's Princess.'

For desperate Diana, what were her chances?
This daring damsel her mum named Frances!

She would find another man to love, that was for sure, as everyone wished for her happiness and contentment. Had she loved her captain in the Guards? Yes, she had, but he had let her down badly.

Carling was Her Darling

After former army captain James Hewitt went on to publicly announce his affair with the Princess, the whole charade was uncovered whereby he answered countless questions by being frank, honest and candid about their physical relationship. He chose royal author Anna Pasternak to edit the recording relating to his five-year dalliance with Diana. Almost five hours of filming went into the episode after which the author, Anna, went to ground exclaiming, 'This will not devastate the Princess in any way.' Even the cameraman was sickened at the leaking of such sordid details. Interviews took place at Hewitt's manor, 'Eversfield,' a five-bedroomed Georgian house near Clovelly in the Devonshire countryside. Miss Pasternak had earlier written 'Princess in Love,' for which she received thousands of pounds in royalties, although the book itself only took five and a half weeks to write. To think the former cavalry officer was doing more than just teaching the young Princes to ride their ponies!

Where would all these discretions end? Further revelations were bound to follow. And then all hell broke loose when 'Squidgygate' emerged – a tape of the Princess talking candidly to James Gilbey, a second-hand car dealer caught off his guard. Someone had picked up the conversation over the air waves and sold it to the papers who went ahead and published the whole caboodle. Apparently, Diana was Gilbey's 'Squidgy' when she could be heard hanging on to his every word. The Princess must have appeared 'squashy' to him at least! She had probably been in love with two James's, but the one who mattered most had been the former cavalry officer whom she completely and utterly adored.

The Princess dodged photographers as best she could, as she tried to get her life back on track. She worked out at a local gym, hoping tough exercise would strengthen her resolve to go on supporting her many charities. She went on television to explain she would be cutting down on her engagements, although she did not want to be marginalized from royal life altogether. Her charities were many and varied, including the British Red Cross, the Royal Marsden and Great Ormand Street Hospital Trusts for children, and the National Aids Trust. She particularly wanted to support children from all walks of life, as she had a natural tendency to be with children.

Of course, she missed her own boys when she was away, but she made up for it by pampering them when she had them to herself at Kensington Palace. William had a crush on Cindy Crawford, the film star, and so she was invited over to meet him. She became quite chummy with her and stayed in contact with Diana throughout. Their apartment at Kensington was on the first floor, with the large sitting room becoming Diana's 'nest' where William could snuggle up to his mother, believing he was looking after her when she was all alone. He was growing up in the midst of history's most controversial divorce and would protect his mother no matter what.

It wasn't by coincidence that another man came into Diana's matrimonial turmoil. The boys had taken up rugby and who should come to call but the dashing rugby captain himself, Will Carling. His dark good looks made Diana swoon with excitement, and she was soon looking forward to his weekly visits to the palace. His rough and tumble with the Princes carried in unremittingly with Diana, as she was besotted by his attention and would want to forget her own predicament whilst they embraced out of the public gaze. She knew he was married and so was she; still, so what did it matter? He brought a new meaning into her life and she craved the excitement of it all. Will was just as besotted with the Princess and was ringing her up all the time. Soon, the press got wind of their entanglement.

When the cat was out of the bag, Carling found himself on the front pages of all the newspapers as well as on the back covers. The rugby captain wasn't amused and shrugged off any suggestion that he was romantically linked with Diana. But his wife was adamant that an affair was in fact going on and promptly left him to his devices. He was ostracised for his behaviour on and off the field and could not get away from his critics. Diana professed her innocence during the whole debacle and vowed never to be drawn into another devious relationship ever again.

The Princess feared new revelations involving Will Carling would shatter any hopes of a good divorce settlement. She appealed to his better judgement for him to deny they were ever lovers. Will's lovely wife knew better than to trust her erring partner and left him in the lurch when he confessed to actually sleeping with Diana. He had promised to stay away from her altogether, but he was caught dropping off presents for William and Harry and then meeting Diana in secret at her sports clinic. When confronted by the press, all he would say was 'she was a good friend.' The situation gave Prince Charles priceless ammunition to be used to reduce Diana's divorce demands. But it had not come to that – yet!

Both Diana and Charles had each confessed to one's infidelity – he with Camilla Parker Bowles and she with James Hewitt. But Charles himself had started the hostilities by having a mistress in the first place. He was likened to his great-great-grandfather, Edward VII who was famous for having had as a mistress the delectable Alice Keppel. And his father before him was guilty of infidelity and lack of inconsideration for his wife. Both kings had travelled intensively, and Edward VII became 'The Peacemaker' when he contrived for the preservation of Europe's peace with France, Germany and other nations.

It was quite a revelation for Camilla Parker Bowles to admit that she was the great-great-granddaughter of Alice Keppel, and it was supposed that she said to Charles, 'Your forebear was sleeping with my forebear, so how about it?' You could say Charles was enamoured by Camilla's frankness in all things, and that is why he fell for her. She flattered herself to think the Prince preferred her company to that of his young wife.

Diana was not going to let their affair drag her down. She sought justification by consenting to having a book published professing to be her own true story of events leading up to her marriage problems. It became Andrew Morton's blockbuster 'Diana – Her True Story,' which portrayed her as a lonely, neurotic Princess, driven to tears and tantrums by an uncaring and adulterous husband. Disclosed was the fact that even on their honeymoon, the Prince was in touch with his long-time companion and mistress, Mrs. Parker Bowles. Much of the material for the book was furnished by Diana's long-time friend, Carolyn Bartholomew who was deemed to know what was what. She explained their fairy tale had come to an end. Diana wanted Charles to leave Kensington Palace, although she took some responsibility for the marriage breaking down. It was Charles who summoned up the courage to ask for a separation, as their partnership had become a tyranny of togetherness that could not be bonded. Diana turned her head when Charles tried to kiss her, and she went alone to the Taj Mahal where she sat contemplating her future. What future was there for a sad Princess?

More sadness would intervene when the death of her father was announced whilst she was skiing in Lech, Austria. She had thought of him constantly and rushed back to be at his bedside. He, who had been in the constant service of the royal family, was now no more and Diana wept bitterly at his loss. If it had not been for her father, the 8th Earl Spencer, equerry to both George VI and the Queen, she would never have met the Prince. Now her brother Charles would become the 9th Earl, and he had troubles of his own. Married to a wife who had suffered the same bulimia as Diana and bringing up four children at Althorp, Charles had a marriage that began to crumble, too, and he was desperate to begin another life abroad in South Africa. Diana went to visit him, but she was too miserable to give him any comfort.

'Camillagate' would not go away. A tape came out of Charles and Camilla engaged in a very intimate conversation. Never-ending embarrassments were the order of the day in the aftermath of these disclosures. Royalty was set for a big shake-up. No less than three of the royal marriages had come to an end.

Ironically, all the royal couples involved had honeymooned on the Royal Yacht Britannia, which had not seemed to be a lucky start. Charles had expressed his concerns in an interview on TV with Jonathan Dimbleby, admitting he had been unfaithful, but only after his marriage to Diana had irretrievably broken down. His affair with Camilla had shaken the monarchy to its foundation, but he had no intention of giving her up.

> The prince loved another – Camilla Parker Bowles
> A married mistress fair – just one of her roles

Diana felt she had been let down – first, by her mother who left her father for another man, then her husband who had had a mistress well before their marriage, and finally, her lover who had revealed all in order to get rich.

She began to feel she was an embarrassment to the royal family, and they would want rid of her. For the children's sake, she and Charles continued for a time to be together, but finally Charles moved his things out of Kensington Palace and into Highgrove for good, where he could be not far from Mrs. Parker Bowles. There, he was at peace with his horses and could join Camilla for gallops throughout the Wiltshire countryside.

'Mrs Parker Bowles is a great friend of mine,' admitted the Prince. 'She's been a friend for a very long time and will continue to be for a very long time.' It was likened to the Duke of Windsor who was willing to give up his throne for the woman he loved. In his case, it was Mrs Wallis Simpson, a divorcee, and the Duke was adamant that their love for each other came first. Soon Camilla would be divorced as her husband had found happiness elsewhere. Apparently, they had been estranged for quite some time whilst their son and daughter were growing up fast.

It took a lot of courage for the Prince to admit he had been unfaithful. 'These things are so personal that it is difficult to know how to talk about them,' he confessed. Diana admitted that she was devastated herself, but she admired his honesty because she thought it took a lot to do that. 'To be honest about a relationship with someone else, in his position – that's quite something,' she declared.

Diana had produced 'an heir and a spare' and so she had done her wifely duty. Now she was free to go! But go where? Surely she had plenty of charities that needed her patronage! Life became very difficult for her. There was a lot she wanted to do but was thwarted by her husband's family. 'They were stopping me,' she maintained. Diana stated on TV the fact that she would not go quietly. Her husband would want to shunt her away, but she had ways and means of getting back at him.

One of the ways was to dress provocatively to let the world know who the best-dressed woman was. The ensemble she chose for this purpose was a stunning black creation split high up on the thigh and revealing one shoulder. Her appearance gave her onlookers quite a shock, as this was not the real Diana. She was showing she did not care about Charles and Camilla and would want them to ride off into the sunset on their enticing stallions!

Meanwhile, Camilla was secure in the knowledge that she had the Prince's heart. She was not bothered about the Duchy of Cornwall income, which provided Charles with £4 million pounds a year, or the Highgrove estate, which included stables and farm buildings. She had her own private income, as Camilla Shand that she once was, was wealthy in her own right.

Charles met Camilla before she wed
With awe he did retreat
But still he loved her, and so it's said
Continued his deceit

Camilla was low profile whereas Diana could be considered high-profile in that her beauty was beyond compare. She was renowned the world over and could pick any man she pleased. Her courage and adversity had turned her into a strong woman, and she had a sense of fun, which folk who came into contact with her found enchanting. She could see more of her friends now, go on holiday and abandon all thoughts of royal protocol.

Camilla was building a new life, too, carrying out renovations on her new retreat – Ray Mill House in Wiltshire that had previously been owned by a wealthy art dealer. She wasn't averse to doing a spot of gardening and could be seen, secateurs in gloved hands, pruning the overgrown shrubs.

Spare the Children

If only royal marriages could be the stuff of Victoria and Albert! They were both twenty, and so in love as never before. Then the poor Queen suffered the loss of her husband at just 42 and was devastated. This consort adapted himself with considerable success to the affairs of state. Queen Victoria was lost without him and must have felt like Diana, not wanting to go on. Even so, she was overseer of the Crimean War, the Indian Mutiny and the Boer War and was proclaimed Empress of India. She gave birth to nine children and was left to soldier on alone after Albert died. She hid herself away for years at her mansion on the Isle of Wight. Of course, royalty was not seen in the light that we see them today. They were aloof and unreachable and, as Diana would observe, not in touch with the common people. How things have changed since the Victorian age. Diana had managed to bridge the gap between the royal family and us. Only she had the ability to touch ordinary people with her love. Yes, Diana was the only link between us and them.

Diana had been the devoted mother, the fashion icon and the wronged woman. She had loved Charles without reserve and now faced the prospect of being divorced from him. There were almost twelve years between them but what had that mattered? She had no credentials but had youth on her side. In time, she became self-assured and sophisticated and had hoped Charles would appreciate her efforts at being nice to all and sundry.

Experience had taught Charles to show little affection and keep a stiff, upper lip, as he realised the monarchy could be damaged irreversibly if he did not divorce and conduct himself with dignity and respect. The Queen had urged this, and, of course, there were the two young Princes to consider. William was a teenager now, and Harry would have to be provided for as he would not succeed to the Duchy revenue, being the younger son. Charles had every intention of filling the role of monarch when the time came. He was fully qualified to become king, possessed a wide knowledge of history and knew more about the divisions of the population than anybody.

The recent scandal of the young royals put the Queen in a very difficult position, as she would be held responsible for the fall of the House of Windsor. How fortunate that she was beyond criticism when it came close to a command that the Prince and Princess divorce without further delay as their separation had lasted more than three years. Diana agreed with a heavy heart as she understood how ordinary people would feel about her ending her marriage, but she hoped they understood how complex and emotional the procedure would be for her. She wanted her son to be king one day, and of course, she would always be his mother. But she held doubts about Prince Charles being a suitable king.

The Queen would be sad to be losing such a prolific daughter-in-law as Diana had proved to be, as she had forged this loving attachment to the people who saw her as Queen of Hearts. She would carry on in this capacity as she had the power of love and understanding of the desperately poor and sick in England and abroad, and she would join campaigns to eliminate poverty and starvation. Only Diana was capable of conducting herself in this capacity. And she was sure the Queen would approve of her new role in society. Underprivileged children would be her number one priority, as she knew just how they felt when they had no-one to care for them.

Diana would seek a £15 million payment in her divorce petition, which was half the original sum demanded by Anthony Julius, the lawyer acting for the Princess. Despite Charles's wealth, he did not have the cash available for a one-off payment. A substantial portion of the Princess's jewellery belonged to the state, but it was estimated that £20 million pounds worth truly belonged to Diana.

She became just 'Diana, Princess of Wales,' and she would continue to be involved in all discussions to do with Prince William and Prince Harry. The Queen had requested a quick settlement to spare the children. Would that it had to be Diana's very own brother-in-law, Robert Fellowes, to get her to respond positively to the Queen!

Diana was now 34 and the Prince 47. She was relinquishing her title 'Her Royal Highness,' and the Prince was still hemmed in by royal restraints. Would this state of affairs bring the prospect of 'Queen Camilla' a little closer? As for Diana, she knew now she would never be Queen. And she realized that, as mother of the future King, she would have to be careful who she dated.

'I have given them everything they want and have played it by the book,' the Princess explained. Diana had an informal meeting with Charles at St James's Palace where they hammered out their proposals. They agreed on property, finance, and most important of all, arrangements for the boys.

It was thought that Diana brokered her own deal, as she wanted the world to know that it was not she who asked for an annulment of her marriage. Since separating from Prince Charles, she had sought the post of roving ambassador for Britain, but the 'old guard' thought her unsuitable for such a role. As it was, she had taken the first step as an ambassador for humanitarian causes, and she launched a £2 billion British Red Cross appeal to help victims of war and famine. Thereto she had sought to present herself as an influential figure in her own right.

Charles had picked up all the bills since their separation. Diana's grooming accounts were excessive – clothes €100,000 annually; personal fitness €12,000; hairdressing €10,000; alternative therapies £8,000; exotic holidays €28,000; and beauty treatments €22,000. Her staff of 20 cost approximately £6,000 per week. Her total yearly expenses could be guessed at about £500,000. Of course, much of Prince Charles's wealth was tied up in assets, but the divorce struck a cruel blow.

Diana maintained her rooms at Kensington Palace. Her apartment included four reception rooms, a dining room, a master bedroom and two guest bedrooms. She felt safe there as it had a £5,000 security system. The palace, a grace and favour residence, set on the western fringes of Hyde Park, was originally bought by William III in 1689 and has other royals in residence.

The Queen's favourite castle, Windsor, suffered a horrifying fire, almost wiping out the 'business end' that included St George's Hall, the 185-ft long great banqueting room, a creation by 19th century architect Jeffry Wyattville. Several of the most important state rooms were damaged, which had been used for gala entertaining. Luckily, the Queen's private apartments were not affected. There she stood, in the midst of the turmoil, a sad and silent figure believing this was not happening. Relics from the flames were being brought out into the open, and folk were on hand trying to save precious paintings and artefacts from the blazing building. It was thought the Queen could well afford the expensive repair bill as she was one of the richest individuals in the country!

For once, the fire took precedence over the official royal duties and helped take the Queen's mind off her children's marriage problems. At least Prince Andrew was by her side, taking charge of the proceedings and helping save countless treasures.

Out of the unhappiness of both Prince Charles and Prince Andrew's marriages came the lovely royal children, and the Queen was euphoric as she loved them intensely. They would accompany her to Sandringham in the summer and Balmoral in the autumn. She just loved having them with her as well as her pet corgis. On the balcony of Buckingham Palace, the young Prince William would salute the way his father does, and the crowds loved it.

Diana was not there any more to acknowledge the crowds. It had been some years since she enraptured those same crowds as she kissed the Prince of Wales after their wedding. That was when everyone thought their romance would last. So it was, too, when Sarah

Ferguson married Andrew and kissed him in front of millions. They both must have known they were in the most prestigious position of having married into the royal family.

Of course, Prince Andrew continued to be in awe of his wife even after they had become a little estranged. He had his own interests, it's true, and Sarah must have felt a little left out. But she had her children's books to write and publish, which took her mind off her problems with Andrew. He just carried on helping to train helicopter pilots whilst Sarah wrote of 'Budgie and His Helicopter' in her spare time. Their relationship worked for a time, and then Sarah longed for holidays abroad and began her quest for becoming the wayward Duchess who liked living life to the full, which greatly impoverished her working husband. She would take her girls, Eugenie and Beatrice, with her wherever she went, and Andrew did not like being the odd man out. This was when he was being cuckolded, as the Duchess was having romantic liaisons with wealthy accomplices from overseas. Prince Andrew turned a blind eye, but beneath it all he was worried sick. He took up golfing and tramped around the 18 holes with a heavy heart. He developed a beautiful swing and an outstanding handicap of 8. He was also keen on photography as this became another of his obsessions, as well as watching TV into the small hours.

The Queen herself seems to have been the happiest person to sustain a good marriage. Philip remained loyal and steadfast and had been constantly at the Queen's side. They had many triumphant trips abroad the Royal Yacht Britannia, and when their children came along, continued with their royal duties. The Queen was tutored by her mother and grandmother from an early age, carrying on the tradition of both women. Her father was known to stammer and was reluctant to become king when his brother gave up the throne for the woman he loved, but he steadfastly took on the role, his wife giving him her support and encouragement that provided him with the inspiration to become a good king. Of his two daughters, Elizabeth was the one to take up the mantle when her time came. As Queen Elizabeth the Second, she has become the ultimate symbol of regality, carrying the Royal House of Windsor into the 21st century with the utmost integrity.

Alas, Diana could not live up to her mother-in-law's expectations. She was out on a limb, experiencing loneliness and frustration. Who would come into her life and transform her unhappiness into joy and contentment? Quite unexpectedly, she was invited to cruise the Aegean Sea on his gigantic ocean-going yacht. He happened to be an Egyptian Mohamed who had met the Princess in the course of his business interests. Mohamed Al Fayed it was who persuaded the Princess she needed a holiday, and he happened to have a yacht at his disposal.

Sell you dresses, Mum

Diana had been one to enjoy the Hospitality of Mohamed Al Fayed when she had previously holidayed on his yacht with the young Princes. She got on well with his wife and they sailed the Mediterranean, lapping up the sunshine up on deck, the Princess diving into the sea for a swim. The paparazzi were not far away, zooming in on the yacht and snapping the Princess unawares. He had a lot to answer for, this Mohamed, who happened to be a millionaire supreme – owning shops, hotels etc. and countless other covetous houses. Yes, you could say he had a hand in everything that made more money for him and his family. But Diana wasn't put off by his wealth. She found him warm and charming, and he made a good impression on her. After all, she shopped at Harrods and he owned that store, too.

Diana had indeed brokered her own deal now that her divorce was imminent. She had a teatime summit at St James's Palace, Charles's official residence, and eventually won a settlement in the region of £17 million. She did not dispute the loss of her title, as all along she wanted to be ordinary and not have to bother with bodyguards and courtiers. Her personal butler, Paul Burrell, who set out her stall almost every day, was sufficient. She became more and more dependent on him, however, and leaned on him when things got a little rough, which they were bound to do when the crowds got a little too close to her. He became, to use Diana's own words, 'my rock,' and was forever by her side wherever she happened to be. He accompanied her to Angola on her landmine campaign, where she was rigged up in protective clothing complete with face visor. Her tall figure, thus attired, stood out from the crowd and the stalwart figure of Paul was never far behind. He had two boys of his own and would take them to the palace to play with William and Harry. He was the one to lay the Princess's clothes out for the next day and arrange her commitments.

Folk were beginning to wonder who the next man in her life would be. A handsome, swarve, good-looking Egyptian maybe! Was there one waiting in the wings? Perhaps she would meet him on a forthcoming cruise! No-one can say it had been arranged. Who was this dark, portly looking stranger holding the Princess's hand?

No less a person than Mohamed Al Fayed's son, the doted-on Dodi, who had met Diana almost ten years before at a polo match. Would these two celebrities be a match for each other? They most certainly were.

He had the reputation of being a playboy. His base was California where he had left a string of girlfriends. One in particular claimed she was engaged to him. Of course, Dodi denied the whole affair when confronting him on the deck of his father's yacht was Diana herself. 'She's for me,' he must have been thinking. Ten exciting days off Saint-Tropez was in the offing. The paparazzi were having a field day snapping the couple smooching away in their deckchairs, oblivious of any snoopers with their long lenses. Diana looked relaxed and ready for romance like she had never looked before. Her worries were behind her as she put her trust in this new fellow who excited her beyond belief. She posed in her bathing costume, her arms held high in the air ready for a dive, and she pitched herself forward ready to drop in the ocean and drown her heavily coiffured highlighted hair.

What did Diana care? She was with the man she loved and everybody could go to hell. She was no longer considered unstable, paranoid or depressed. She had found a new love!

Diana's despair had been raked over numerous times by her followers, and, now that she was at her beguilingly beautiful best, they seemed to be burrowing more and more into her very soul. She had inherited a piece of her father's fortune, so she wasn't badly off, although she did not possess huge personal wealth. Charles did not intend on marrying again, but Diana always thought it a possibility that she would find someone and go on to have more children.

The auction of her clothes in New York was a tremendous success. The event brought together the fashion houses who had had the pleasure of dressing the most famous icon of the 20th century. To think it had been Prince William's suggestion to auction this couture collection for charity. Cancer, AIDS and the Royal Marsden Hospital all benefited from this sale of 79 dresses once worn by the Princess. Five thousand people, including celebrities, viewed the clothes, and one even went to the Franklin Mint to be used in a competition.

In the meantime, Diana was getting heavily involved with her serious new love, and she was about to cruise the Mediterranean once more with this attentive new beau.

His full name was Emad al Fayed, and the minute they got engrossed in conversation, it was as if they had known each other before and were re-kindling a lost romance. He made sure Diana had everything she wanted on the cruise, as below deck were ostentatious living and dining quarters, plus opulent sleeping accommodation for guests of noble birth, just in case a prince or princess happened to be cruising along with the family!

Dodi had only to snap his fingers and the staff would respond immediately, pouring drinks and providing light snacks as he and Diana lazed up on the deck, their cares far away, except that Diana thought of her boys and wished they were aboard enjoying the same companionship as she was. Dodi most certainly thought of the girl he had left behind in California, a certain Kelly Fisher who he had been dating for several months. They had met at the Ritz Paris, and he had taken her to see where the Duke and Duchess of Windsor had lived in the Bois de Boulogne, which Dodi's father now owned.

It wasn't coincidence that Dodi had in mind to show Diana the same mansion when they eventually got to Paris after their cruise. All this time, Kelly was awaiting Dodi's return to her at Paradise Cove where they planned to live after they were married. He had made the excuse to go to Paris saying he missed his two Schnauzer dogs, though

Kelly realised later that it was to see his latest love – Princess Diana.

Kelly explained when she knew she had been ditched for Diana. 'Dodi was wonderful on the phone, calling me four or five times a day. He once sent me 500 roses,' she gushed, 'as well as inundating me with Harrods teddy bears. He was quiet and let other people do the talking.' Dodi would often stay at his £3,000- a-night bungalow at the exclusive Beverly Hills Hotel.

Diana would have done well to have gone to the States with him to enjoy his colossal wealth in that sunshine paradise. But she had to be content with languishing on his father's yacht and seeing Sardinia instead of Sunset Strip. Of course, she had been to the States and met the President and this lady – and made a good impression you might be sure!

Would Diana have been at home in Paradise Cove, the celebrated colony to the north of Malibu? A villa decked out with vine leaves, an Olympic size swimming pool, four-poster beds draped over by cascades of organza, and complete with sweeping staircase for her to glide down when she was in a happy mood? No, she would sigh her Scarlett O'Hara sigh, and be more contented behind the walls of Balmoral with her boys.

She realised Dodi had been married, albeit for just a few months, to Susanna Gregard, but this lady did not appreciate his life of luxury and left after just eight months. She had dragged Dodi off to see a psychic to see if they were suited to each other, but the consultation failed to reveal that their brief marriage would soon be over.

By a quirk of fate, Diana did the very same thing – took Dodi off to a little-known place in Derbyshire in order to get him 'vetted.' They were seen landing in their helicopter for a consultation with 'Romany Rita' who told them a thing or two about their relationship. Most folk want to know if they will ever get rich, but Diana most probably wondered if the psychic could shed any light on what the future held for her.

From the place to Pilsley they flew
Di and her Playboy anew
With their love still so buoyant
They see a clairvoyant and
Are snapped sneaking back to the crew

Someone managed to video Diana and Dodi running for their
'get-away copter.' It was supposed to have been an informal visit, but
folk soon got wind of just who it was dropping in by helicopter. The
pair of them looked happy enough as they held hands and ran back
to their crew.

She felt 'newly loved'

How daunting for Diana if she only knew the truth! Was Dodi planning to give her a ring? Maybe she hoped to have a child! All that contentment had made her have a rounded tummy. 'I'm beginning to feel really loved,' she told her friend, Rosa Monckton, who had shared a recent holiday with Diana in Greece, confirming the view that Diana was just enjoying this new romance, but did not intend it to go too far. 'I'm having a wonderful time, but the last thing I need is a new marriage.' She went on, 'I need it like a bad rash on my face.'

She was desperate to get back to her boys. Dodi accompanied Diana off the boat, barefooted and barely able to see as the cameras flashed them in the face in an effort to take them unconventionally. They were headed back to Paris where the Ritz was preparing for their arrival. Dodi wanted to show off this most photographed, most loved and most famous person in the world, and she was right there, by his side.

It seemed like they were a fairy-tale couple, which indeed they were at this juncture of their lives. Diana did indeed feel loved for the first time. 'I feel newly loved,' and 'Dodi is a fantastic man,' she gushed on the phone to her fine friend, Cindy Crawford.

Everyone was looking into Dodi Fayed's credentials. He was known to be the film producer son of controversial businessman Mohamed AI Fayed. He had been a graduate of Sandhurst Military Academy and a former London officer for the United Arab Emirates. Needless to say, he also had a penchant for fast cars and beautiful women.

And so Diana would be his last beautiful woman. She would want this romance to go its full course. But she had William and Harry to think about and would not want their future to be jeopardised by her new man. And Charles would not be very pleased, either, at having her run off with an Egyptian. He probably feared for her safety right there and then.

M. Paul, driver of the ill-fated Mercedes, was found to have 175 milligrams of alcohol per 100 millilitres of blood in his system at the time of the fateful crash. There was no doubt about it – Diana was killed by a drunk driver whilst being driven from the Ritz Paris to Dodi's apartment across Paris. Although chased by the paparazzi on motorcycles, they were in no way to blame for the mishap, as when they caught up, they tried to do what they could for the car occupants.

> Her heart was crushed – her soul destroyed
> What was she doing without her boys
> Motherless now – they sought to grieve
> 'Twas hard to fathom – hard to believe!

Diana's devoted butler brought along the formal, long-sleeved black dress purchased a few weeks previously for her to be buried in. 'England's Rose' would be mourned in style and majesty, for she was without a doubt the most memorable Princess never to have become a Queen. Diana had died and how the world mourned. She had had her last fling and paid the price. She had sparkled like a diamond and now the allure had diminished with her death at just 36. Our bold Princess would be laid to rest with the most profound grief and sorrow.

> So thank-you Lord for giving us Diana
> Fair of face, so polite in manner
> We won't forget her charming presence
> Her sparkling charm – her effervescence

This courageous girl will be forever etched in our memories as we all carry on with our mundane tasks and our everyday chores. She has gone to green pastures and will be watched over as she rests on her island paradise.

Mother Theresa had given Diana a rosary, and this was placed over her body in the coffin. Soon, a tide of flowers would be on their way for the saddest-ever funeral of our Princess of Wales.

White lilies would grace her coffin, the solemn flower of bereavement. There was more sorrow over the loss of this Princess than any other royal before her. She was in her prime when she was so cruelly taken from us.

How many other celebrities died at 36? Marilyn Monroe, for one, who died from an overdose. Elton John commemorated her death by composing 'Candle in the Wind.' Now he would have to change the words round a bit to make the song fitting for Diana. The two of them had been buddies, attending the funeral of fashion icon Versace only a few weeks previous to Diana's demise. Now, countless prayers would be uttered, and thousands of candles lit, as Diana was the icon ensuring her own immortality, as she will be eternally young.

AIDS victims will recall how Diana held their hands in their moment of desperation. She suffered all the little children to come unto her, and they did, in their hundreds. She picked them up and hugged them to her like no other royal had done before. And she loved to comfort the terminally ill, giving them assurance that there was someone who cared in their darkest hours. Because of her never-ending crusades for the poor and undernourished, she was being grieved with the utmost sorrow and poignancy. They were giving her back the love she had given them unconditionally. As the funeral procession headed down the Mall, both sides were lined by those very people. Three generations of the Windsor line walked quietly at the head of the procession. They were Prince Charles, Prince Philip, Earl Spencer and the unforgettable spectacle of the two young Princes, William and Harry. Folk fell about crying at the sight of the boys, looking so dignified as they mourned their mother. They were all in dark suits, and all in step, following the coffin that was decked in white tulips, white roses and white lilies. Above the silent footsteps could be heard a lone piper playing 'Abide with Me.' There were miles to go before the final resting place of Diana. The hearse was continually being bombarded with flowers thrown at it all the way to Althorp. Every so often, the hearse had to stop in its tracks and the strewn flowers wiped from the windscreen. At long last, it reached its destination and the ornate gates of Althorp closed behind the cortege. Diana was home, but of course this was the Spencers' home and not the Windsors'. This shining star had been in their midst though they did not know it. Our Queen of Hearts was laid to rest on the Round Oval, set in a lake. Earl Spencer was looking after Diana in return for her having looked after him. This most memorable woman, her compassion for ordinary people, her informality, and above all, her beauty, will be forever perpetuated by all who came to knew her, and her kindred spirit will haunt the palaces of the royals for ever more.

The Princess was asked whether she regretted never being Queen. 'Yes, yes,' she answered, 'we would have been the best team in the world. I could shake hands until the cows came home. And Charles could make serious speeches.'

Yes indeed, Diana would have made a good Queen. She was endeared to her public by her strength of character and vibrant personality. She was able to communicate warmth and compassion and make those less fortunate than herself feel loved and wanted. She never believed in her own beauty in spite of all the compliments paid to her for over two decades.

'Someone's got to go out there and love people and show it – I myself can do it,' Diana professed, 'because I don't go by the book, I lead from the heart.' Her way of doing things differently appealed to the people and is why she became known as 'The People's Princess.' 'I'd like to be Queen, but in a different way, in people's hearts,' she declared. She knew she was capable of giving love to those who needed it, even if it was for just an hour, just a day, or a minute even. Diana knew she fitted the unique role of giving the poor and deprived her love and attention. She had become the most successful fundraiser in the country, and she had been associated with 150 charitable causes. By far the most important of her fundraising activities had been the sale of her own dresses at Christie's in New York. The event was of interest worldwide, with everyone fighting for possession of at least one of her ensembles. The gowns were all meticulously catalogued and raised millions of pounds. All the famous designer names were up there, including Rifat Ozbek, Amani, Bruce Oldfield, Zandra Rhodes and Elizabeth Emanuel.

Knowing Diana affected those who had sought to interview her throughout her two decades of being in the limelight. Particularly so for James Whitaker who almost shadowed the Princess and got to know her more like a friend than a target of his gossip columns. She was, he said, 'a truly inspirational woman, and her awareness of him touched him to the core. He did not know how he would live without her, as he had followed her up mountains where she could steal him an interview in between skiing down the pistes.

Of course, this was after she had separated from the Prince, and he was concerned for her safety, especially as she had dumped her Scotland Yard bodyguards. She felt it gave her more space to be without them. 'Do you worry about me a lot?' She enquired of her follower. 'Yes,' replied Whitaker, 'I wish you had kept your security.' He went on, 'I fear something might happen to you one day.' 'Would you come to my funeral of I were to die?' the Princess enquired. James was shocked at this question, spoken with candid simplicity. 'Yes, I would, but you are a lot younger than me, and I would be retired, if not dead already, by the time you die.' Diana persisted, 'Why would you want to come to my funeral?' and waited for Whitaker's response. 'For two reasons,' he replied, 'the first, to report and record your death, and secondly, because you are an astonishing lady who often confuses me but always intrigues. It is an event I could not miss.'

How ironic that the Princess was to die four years after this incident. Whitaker felt their lives were inextricably intertwined and did not wish his world to continue without Diana being a part of it. He found her to be unspeakably charming and stated that she had charisma coming out of every pore. He had not witnessed the kind of compassion that Diana possessed, nor the great sense of humour she had. Indeed, she rose above adversity and changed the way we regard the royals. Yes, she tore down the regal edifices in one fell swoop.

Even the Queen had to bow to public demands and fly the flag from the palace at half-mast. The Royal Standard had never flown at half-mast before, but mounting public anger made the palace change its attitude.

There had been no light at the end of the tunnel for Diana. She had paid the price of being so popular in that senseless Paris car crash. They chose 'The King of Love My Shepherd Is' as one of the hymns close to her heart. Not since V.E. Day in 1945 had London seen such huge crowds. They had waited hours in order not to miss the funeral procession of their Princess. Diana would have been proud indeed. She had endured two decades of public life and could now rest in peace. No more to dance with the likes of John Travolta and Wayne Sleep or perhaps her lost Prince Charming. She had been there, done that. No-one knew she could play the piano, either, as she had kept her talents under wraps.

She let it be known that Prince William would make a good king. 'Britain will be lucky to get William,' she emphasized. 'He's all right.' Even if Diana was destined never to become queen, her son will most certainly become a king of the utmost integrity and refinement because he is his mother's son in looks as well as deportment.

Poor Diana, she never had a chance to become a roving ambassador for Britain. She was taken from us in that deplorable crash. The Parisian tunnel will have a lot to answer for in the years to come. The man by her side died almost immediately, and his family buried him quickly and quietly away from the public's gaze. He must be remembered for giving our Princess a good deal of happiness in her final weeks. They may even have married, given time, as who knows what was on their minds in the events leading up to their deaths.

The pursuit in Paris had come to a sudden stop, and with it, the hopes and dreams of a profound Princess. Our 'days of Diana' were over for good. Whatever would the world do without her? Her death was on everyone's conscience. No-one could have foreseen it. It was like a bombshell. It devastated everyone to the depths of their souls. 'Diana is dead' echoed around every corner of the globe.

It had been flags and flowers all the way to Althorp. The 'goddess of hunting' was laid to rest. She would be hounded no more. What a life to end at just 36 years. There were never-ending condolences sent to Kensington Palace. Masses of flowers caused a tide outside the palace gates. There were poems galore on tiny scraps of paper. Maybe someone would take time to read them and then pass them on to the two Princes.

How would the fashion houses cope now that they had no Diana to dress? There would be no future engagements to plan, no charities to sponsor, no efforts made to remain slim and be in the public eye.

Yes – the last bouquet had been thrust into Diana's hands, the last handshakes had been pressed, the last flash had gone off taking her photograph, and the last entrance and departure made to the sound of crowds cheering and clapping.

No more jostling for position to see Diana appear, no more necks craning for a better view, and no Diana to live to see in the new millennium. Her last meal had been eaten, her last drink relished, and her last holiday enjoyed. No more trips abroad, and no more phone calls exclaiming 'It's Disco Di from K.P.' She died being her own beautiful self, sophisticated and svelte, and she had lost consciousness beside her romantic beau who had ceased to be. Not to see her sons grow up would be her greatest sorrow. To think of them growing up into handsome young men without their mother is too sad for people to contemplate. The boys will miss Diana's hugs and kisses, and most of all, her spontaneity.

The press felt bereaved without Diana to report on every day. Who could possibly fill her place? How did her mother feel without this youngest daughter who became so loved by her public? And her sisters, too, will miss her charming company. Her brother Charles had heaped praise on his sister by declaring 'she was unique – she understood the most precious needs of human beings, particularly those who suffered.'

Diana and Charles had been 'sixties children' running wild and free within the royal Sandringham estate, exchanging frolics with the royal Princes. They were full of fun and high spirits. Charles Spencer was grateful to have had Diana look out for him during those pristine years, and now he could watch over her peaceful island of rest, as she had to come home, to his place.

In the words of Keats – Diana will remain forever young, forever fair. How fitting for our perfect Princess who was never to become Queen.

www.ingramcontent.com/pod-product-compliance
Lightning Source LLC
Chambersburg PA
CBHW051816050726
47598CB00006B/2592